Self Treatments

including

The Radiant I AM

Self Treatments

including

The Radiant I AM

by

Emma Curtis Hopkins
2nd edition

WiseWoman Press

Self Treatments, including The Radiant I AM,
2nd edition
by Emma Curtis Hopkins, 1849-1925

With illustrations by
Rev. Shirley Lawrence, pastor emeritus,
Sanctuary of Truth, Pasadena, CA.

1st edition published, 2007
By WISEWOMAN PRESS
Portland, Oregon
ISBN: 978-0-945385-14-1

2nd edition published, 2025
By Portal Center Press
www.portalcenterpress.com
ISBN: 978-1-936902-60-6

Religion/Spirituality.
Metaphysics.

From the author…

Keep this book in your own possession.

Learn its contents by heart.

Let it be one article never handled by any fingers but your own, never seen by any eyes but your own.

One day you will discover that you are born again.

Contents

Preface	i
Foreword to the 1st edition	v
Soul Speech	1
Self-Treatment	7
The New Gospel	71
Affirmations	77
Forgiveness	83
A New Covenant	85
The Radiant I AM	91

Preface

This is the 2nd edition of this little book, which has been remarkably popular in the 15 years since it was first published.

When we put it together, back in 2010, we combined Emma's most well-known journal entries with a few of the treatment guidelines that she offers in the later versions of her textbook: Scientific Christian Mental Practice, and High Mysticism.

For this new edition, since we've had the opportunity to work with many more volumes of Emma's writings, we've added a piece from her *Judgement Series:* her vivid description of the difference between the speech of the intellect and the speech of the soul – with her encouragement to learn to recognize and allow the Soul to speak.

Now, for all the wonderful teaching and writing that beloved Emma offered so many, there were far too many times when she, like the rest of us, felt separated from the divine. But, unlike most of us, she knew what to do. She knew that the words she used with feeling, from the heart and her very Soul, must give her what they claimed. She knew, also, that what she thought, spoke, and wrote down from those depths had to become her experience.

And so we have the gift of her heart-felt thoughts and words, her very own Soul-speech available to us, today, 100 years after her passing.

May you, too, find the power she and so many of her students found...

>Ruth L. Miller,
>Managing editor
>Portal Center Press
>2025

Foreword to the 1st edition

When Emma Curtis Hopkins was teaching, she encouraged her students to use a daily journal to record three things:
1. their ideas of good
2. their praise and gratitude
3. the healings and transformations that resulted from their treatments.

So it's not too surprising that, among the papers remaining from her seminary in Chicago, were found journals containing records of her own daily practice.

From these, her students gleaned the remarkable pieces of consciousness-raising practice that have become known as "Self-treatment" and "The Radiant I Am." These were typed up, mimeographed, and handed down from one generation of students to the next, as precious gems to be shared with someone who would understand.

And understanding them is no easy task. To the reader lacking the context of her twelve lessons, the ideas presented here may seem rather strange. They assume a worldview that is in accord with the gospel of the New Testament, but which is rarely taught in Christian churches. Within that worldview, they are designed to free the person speaking them or writing them from the bondage of old ideas of lack and separation, and expand our awareness of the power and possibilities promised to us in the new covenant established by Jesus the Nazarene.

Then, both pieces are written in Emma's self-described "complicated way of explaining" herself. She was a Victorian schoolteacher, growing up at the height of Ralph Waldo Emerson's popularity and modeling her rhetorical style on his. More, drawing heavily on the King James edition of the Bible, she sometimes slips into that style of English. Nonetheless, repeated reading—aloud if possible—leads to deeper understanding, and empowerment.

In the first selection, simply called "Self-Treatment," beloved Emma provides a brief overview of the lessons that she taught so many times in so many ways to thousands of people from the late 1880s through the early 1920s. In this outline, she helps us to release any ideas that have limited us and provides a radically new basis for understanding the gospel.

A few of the treatments that this great "teacher of teachers" offered her students are included, following this powerful summary. These are drawn from her books and lectures, and appropriately cited.

In the final selection, we see her own personal treatment, probably a Friday morning practice, designed to lift the writer/speaker out of any limiting patterns of thought into the state of consciousness that Emma called "High Mysticism."

Emma Curtis Hopkins

These pieces have empowered hundreds of practitioners and ministers to step beyond their normal thought patterns and become "centers" of healing and transforming energy—for themselves and all those around them.

One of the centers that have maintained these teachings over the past century was the Sanctuary of Truth in Pasadena, California. There, Reverend Shirley Lawrence was instrumental in ensuring that these works were not lost to the world, and her sketches illustrate this little book.

All of us at WiseWoman Press trust that you will find these treatments for the self to be as useful and powerful as have the many who have treasured and used them for the past hundred-plus years.

Blessings on your journey...

Rev. Michael Terranova,
managing editor
Rev. Dr, Ruth L. Miller,
designing editor
2007

Soul Speech[1]

---

[1] From *The Judgement Series,* WiseWoman Press, 2008

Foreword *Self Treatments*

The wise men of all countries have sought to look upon their Soul, their own "I AM." When you find them able to lay down their body and take it up again at will, you may know they have found their own Soul, their Jesus Christ, undescribed, sinless "I AM." When you find them able to turn thoughts from sick thoughts into well thoughts at will, then you may know they have found their own Soul, their Jesus Christ, unhypnotized "I AM." When you find them doing these things, and then not doing them, yet trying to do them, you may know they are still being whiffled in the delusion of pairs of opposites. They have not found their own will.

The Buddhists have 600 million believers because so many of them have almost seen their Soul.

The Muslims have 200 million believers because so many truths have been spoken of each man's own God Soul.

The Christians have 400 million believers because they describe one man who found His own soul; who stood on Hattin Heights and notified the race of men what their rights are and were and forever shall be—not as intellect molding human events with painful struggles, but as Soul, God, shining on whomsoever it will—in whatsoever fashion it will, unhinderable, undefeatable, unspeakable Light.

There are six Bibles which bring forward the axiomatic principles of the Soul as man has caught glimpses of it and reported what he has seen, felt, realized. They tell the Truth as far as the intellects of the writers were windows open enough to let Truth be told. Fix upon one of these Bibles at a time, and at the end of the reading of them, choose which one has turned you backward towards your own "I AM" with most powerful pushes. Read that one three times over.

These Bibles are:
- Christian Bible
- Hindu Bhagavad-Gita
- Chinese Tao-te-King
- Egyptian Book of the Dead
- Mohammedan Al-Koran
- Zoroastrian Zend Avesta

Know, however, that no bible is equal to Soul speech.

Spiritual Science means Christ Jesus speaking; or the speech of the Soul in all men, which has been called Christ. It starts out with the statement of the Presence of God everywhere, the Power of God everywhere, the Science God everywhere.

There is no direction in which we can turn but that fronting us is our own Soul, or our own God. There is nothing we can know like knowing God, the Presence, Power, Science, that takes us from sight of delusions to sight of undeluded Soul.

Self-Treatment

I

A treatment is not something to bring about in life or affairs or mind or body, something that was not already in life, in affairs, in mind, in body, before.

A treatment is a Truth stated. Whatever happens when Truth is stated happens because Truth was not manifest till it was stated. It touches the principle announced by John, the beloved disciple, that without the spoken Word of Truth, the manifested God is not possible.

The man of religion must have an orderly arranged statement of principles to which he subscribes.

The man of religion keeps one treatment in his mind constantly. It is a truth. That word is "God."

A word is a treatment.

Whenever he describes God. he gives the whole world a treatment; not to be aware that God is, but to make the right statement of God is the first treatment of religion.

The first lesson of Spiritual Science is the statement of the first principle taught by pure and undefiled religion. It is this: The Name, or God, omnipresent, omnipotent, omniscient. Good, Sprit, Mind.[2]

The second lesson is the second principle. It is this: Denial of all but God.

The third lesson is the third principle. It is this: Affirmation of all as God.

---

[2] Throughout Emma's works, words that describe God or name qualities or aspects of the divine are always capitalized.

The fourth lesson is the fourth principle. It is this: Faith is the evidence that God is all.

The fifth lesson is the fifth principle. It is this: Works are the rest of mind in the presence of God.

The sixth lesson is the sixth principle. It is this: Understanding of God is the only understanding worthwhile.

The seventh lesson is the seventh principle. It is this: Birth or bringing forth is sight of God in all things everywhere and seeing God only. This is possible.

The eighth principle is Sight or the Spiritual mind, which is never deceived.

The ninth is Holiness, which is the only nature of all things. There is no sin by this principle. The confession of sin is only the pouring out of secret opinions concerning ignorance, inefficiency and shortcomings which have no part nor lot in God. Our only adversary is God. The only opposition we meet is the presence of God, the inconvincible One. "Behold I am against thee, saith the Lord."

The tenth is the discussion of Forgiveness, which in Science is giving for secret misapprehension of self the divine apprehension of Self. Then in mysticism is the divine Self one in all, as the inconceivably small point everywhere present.

The eleventh is Judgment.

The twelfth is Praise.

These twelve are the only subjects ever discussed by religion or metaphysics. They all mean one Name. It is the Name that is not yet spoken. It is in thy heart. It was with thee in the beginning, it is with thee now, it will be forever with thee. It rusheth through the universe.

No science has it written out. No man hath spoken it aloud. No man hath whispered it. It is the unspeakable Name.

The name Jesus Christ held as a breath sinks down into the heart and turns and overturns the mind that is seated there on its throne till below all and more energetic than all that man has known, thought or felt before, it tells a language new and strange. The mystic word unspeakable is in the heart which lets the name Jesus Christ into it. A light like a lamp of smokeless fire burns from that Name.

The first treatment must forever be a name.

The name God is not the true name of the ineffable One from whom we came forth.

Self-treatment *Self Treatments*

Did we not have our home somewhere? Remember from whence ye came forth. Remember now thy Creator in the days of thy youth or now as thou art first setting forth in Science of Mind Eternal.

Now is the time to remember. The mathematician says he does not take up new calculations but remembers what he once knew. Some preachers remember some far away place and time when they spoke powerfully. Some people can half catch glimpses of a supernal light from whence they came long hence in the past.

Are we not as they that dream while we do not remember—remember—from whence we came forth?

The Hindus have their devotees remember books by heart that they may somewhere catch the clue of their beginning, their home whence they sprang forth.

He who shall remember the Name of that from whence he sprang shall be It.

The name God does not bring the memory. The names of God do not one of them bring it. They do however seem to stir the memory, for memory is a path to something over some words.

One name of that which is the Spirit and Life is Jesus Christ. It is both God and man. It is the indecomposable element. It hath nothing of which it is composed or for which it stands. It is Itself and speaks a language to the heart, as an independent potentiality. It is the mystic Name in that it gives an understanding of the "I" of man. It gives an understanding of God. It gives an under-standing of Science. It gives the unspeakable Name. We cannot get that Name except by it. We soon see that it is to the eye, lips, ears, and mind one name but to the great fact of being it is another. It is the statement of that purpose that is working now with us. Thus it is the statement of truth. It is therefore a treatment.

It takes the hearing and leads it back to the altar fire from whence all hearing started and touches it with a flake of some power the hearing had never before caught. Nothing can hinder the hearing caught at the altar fires. It is born of God.

"Whatsoever is born of God overcometh the world."

Sight, beauty, strength, wisdom, lighted by one touch of divine fire cannot be stopped or limited.

Emma Curtis Hopkins

This Name takes the whole mind back to its fountainhead step by step. The Name—The Name!

Whose voice sounds on my hearing when Jesus Christ is spoken, is thought, is breathed? What home glimpses on some topless heights where my sight beyond sight stretches?

Whatsoever is born of that fire is born of God.

Whosoever is born of that Name finds himself at home, finds his God, finds his life, finds his love, finds his mind, finds truth.

He speaks one Name, and understanding by and through it all other names, finds himself to be the unspoken One. Finding himself by this pathway he has found all that is to be found. He is satisfied.

Om is not the name.

Isis is not it.
Osiris is not it.
God is not it.

Omnipresence, Omnipotence, Omniscience are but cloaks that smother, but Jesus Christ is the truth that uncovers—unclothes—exposes what was and is and ever shall be free.

A name is a treatment. There is none other name given that in itself is understanding of all save One known among men by the name Jesus Christ. That giveth understanding of that One whose name is One unspeakable. Sit thou on the right hand with that Name till understanding shines.

II

The Prince of this world cometh and findeth nothing in me.

The Prince of this world is that which the world seeth and striveth to be one with in order that success may crown their days.

The Prince of this world ordaineth the slaughter of animals to feed men.

Therefore he who slaughtereth most animals shall be greatest on some line in the kingdom where this Prince reigneth.

He ordaineth the kings and emperors of this world.

Therefore that emperor or king who killeth most and setteth his heel most vengeantly on the necks of people is most in favor on some line with the Prince whose motto is: *"Captivity is my Name."*

"I am God and there is none beside me."

"I set kings in their places."

"I ordain the land animals to prey and the sea fish to devour."

"I harden the hands and hearts of whom I will and they do my bidding every one."

"I am evil. He who is most evil is most like me."

Now this Prince cometh to Jesus Christ and findeth nothing of his own substance in Him—nothing!

And Jesus Christ fearlessly looking the whole size of evil squarely in the face seeth nothing of His own substance in the Prince of this world.

He taketh this Prince, by his supreme name, which is Captivity, by the neck and leadeth him into oblivion.

His name is then forgotten. He who hath most forgotten evil is he who hath most dominion. Jesus Christ hath led Captivity captive. Jesus Christ hath put Satan behind Him into the oblivion of entire forgetfulness. Jesus Christ cometh squarely up to the whole realm of sorrow, pain, spoliation, trouble and seeth nothing in it.

"Depart from Me, I never knew you."

There is nothing in the Prince of this world whose name is Captivity—nothing.

There is no reigning power. There is no substance. There is no life. There is no truth. There is no love. There is nothing to the Prince who ordaineth the abuse of men. Nothing of him who slayeth. Nothing that can hurt or make afraid. There is nothing to fear.

Know ye not that the Father hath committed all power, all substance, all judgment, all this world unto His only begotten Son, Jesus Christ, Prince of Peace, Good Will to men? King of Glory, Love Incarnate, The Righteous, The Redeemer, Lord of Lords and Very God of Very God.

"Be not afraid, ye believe in God, believe also in Me." I have overcome the world. I now reign. Let all the isles rejoice. Let the mountains sing praises.

Who is there that findeth his love in Me?

Who findeth all that he is in Me? Who is there that looketh at the Prince of this world, at him that ordained the dominion of hurt and fear and findeth nothing in him?

Nothing at all? He is Mine and I am his. I have put My Name upon him. I have made My abode in him. The Prince of this world that succeedeth by force, cometh hoping to find some of his own substance in him that hath Me abiding in him and findeth nothing—nothing. So he that is Mine hath no hurt. He that terrifieth cannot find a portion in him that hath Me in him which tendeth to death or cruelty or anger or fear. So he leaveth him forever. Behold I live and they that find all in Me live also! I Jesus Christ have led Captivity captive.

III

A man is known by the company he keeps. To be aware that thou art in the presence of an attentive mind unto whom thou canst address thyself will show thee the word and the work of that mind.

"The Son can do nothing; only what He seeth the Father do. And what things so-ever He doeth these doeth the Son also."

Tip thy speech with healing fire by speaking much to the attentive Presence near thee. Tip thy pen with irresistible light by writing thy pages to the Eternally Wise overlooking thy truth.

Enchant thy manners with splendid graces by remembering that thou art in the everlasting company of the Perfect One.

Gird thy loins with strength by acknowledging that the Almighty is thy ally.

The word and the work of the enlightened stand equally in favor with mankind. If thou canst speak so as to give thy neighbor one taste of bliss as thou recallest unto him one slightest memory of the Paradise from whence he first came out, he will take slight heed of whether thou canst heal the sick or raise the dead.

If thou canst make bread out of nothing like St. Franchy in the seventh century, if thou canst cure those born deformed, thou wilt give a drop of the elixir of joy to all who see thee work. It will remind them of the heavenly place of light from whence they came out. They will not ask thee to talk.

By word or by work are the enlightened recommended unto the world. The enlightened are those who remember most of the country of delight where their soul was nerved with happiness before they said that they forgot the way back to God. They are those who believe the attentive Mind bends over them and unto It they address themselves.

They do not think it a far away country of wisdom. They say that it is nigh at hand. Yea, they have even seen that the whole land of Paradise was in their own body smiling as a face and kind as the bliss of mother love. Watching a face, its whole character is revealed to thee.

Where is the face of the Absolute God? "It is nigh thee—very nigh." It is even in and through thy whole body. What sayest thou unto that face? That which thou sayest it answereth back again. The Mind that attendeth unto thee is one Mind. It has one language.

It is not necessary that thou talk to thy neighbor man about his health; talk to that Mind attentive to thy speech in the language that it would use if thou couldst hear it speak on the subject of thy neighbor's health.

If thou speakest to thy neighbor thou wilt be like that neighbor. If thou speakest to a mind that is silly thou shalt be silly. If thou speakest to Absolute Wisdom thou art Absolute Wisdom indeed while thou art addressing that Mind. Thou art known by thy Friendship.

IV

The Hindus repeat whole books by heart striving thereby to remember what their soul knows. Sometimes their repetitions have the wished for effect and they have a realization of some one point as their enlightened sages have given it. From that moment they remember some other happy truth and then another till they also are called sages.

All the Bibles of the nations are memories of these sages. When they have remembered certain principles which they formerly knew they have disappeared from human view. Men have then said that they are ascended into light or into Paradise or into Heaven from whence we all came forth. All the memorizing we do of any man's words takes us back as on a golden thread to our point in life where he and we were much alike. The recollection of his words brings on its string his peculiarities and idiosyncrasies. We know them. We either copy them or drop them. As we copy them we cease to be like ourselves and for the while we are copying his mind—we have ceased to go back to our soul point.

Remembering the words of Jesus Christ we take fewest earthly notions along. Indeed we are told He communicates no guile along the threads of His matchless eloquence. He leads mind by His Name back to the fountain where words were born—where abilities were born—where genius began. Then our words are born again. No matter what they then say they accomplish wonders.

"I will give thee a mouth and wisdom so that no man is able to gainsay nor resist thee."

Our actions count as noble successes and nothing can resist their success.

Success gives a taste of bliss and entire bliss is heaven. Each taste of happiness is a reminder of heaven. "Whatsoever is born of God overcometh the world."

Laying our words back upon the anvil from whence power is born is laying them on the altar. Laying our will back upon the substance from whence the Divine Will moves is laying our will upon the altar. Laying our money back upon the solid light from whence prosperity is born is laying our money back upon the altar.

Words, will, money, from the altar have miraculous energy.

John Grande of Spain (1759) fed multitudes by putting a piece of meat and bread before the image of the Virgin Mary and after that the more he gave to the famine-stricken people the more he had.

It is plain that he had put his words, will and possessions back into the fountain Mind called God and placing the bread and meat before the Virgin was then a successful act.

Born of God—Born of God—Born of God!

The thoughts that thou usest are will-o'-the-wisps till they have been laid back on the Mind that is God. Then they are kindled with a new fire. They are come to life. They can work.

Actions are pantomimes till they have been kindled on the altar where power and life and light are real. As a name stops the click of the will-o'-the-wisp thoughts and begins to turn their wheels backward toward the soul point where the electric fires of God are burning, so a truth strikes again and again on the electric fires of Soul.

Born of God—Born of God—Born of God!

My thoughts are born of God. My words are born of God. My will is born of God. My actions are born of God. This is truth. It is a touch of my will-o'-the-wisp thoughts on reality to say they are born of God.

God is here. I touch my face against God and its beauty is the beauty of God. I lay my gold on God's here substance and its purchasing power is the Jesus Christ ability.

God is here. Behind me is God. I lay all I have there and say unto it—"Born of God!"

God is before me. I put down all that I have there and say unto it—"Born of God!"

On the right I stretch my hand and lay it upon God—and lo! My hand is born of God. It works whatsoever is good.

On the left hand there is my resting place.

Under me is the eternal God.

My feet touching God go not astray.

I remember where I am and born of God I am all God.

V

The only difference between inferior people and superior people (so-called) is in their ability to concentrate to an idea. Every idea carries its own quality. We do not have to compel an idea to be itself. It is itself.

So when we attend strictly to an idea it will infuse and diffuse and interpenetrate itself into us till it is us.

A noble, a lofty, a sublime idea being attended unto infuses, diffuses, interpenetrates till we are it and it only. Half attention makes partial likeness. Slight attention is remoteness indeed.

Trainers of animals select only those which can look steadfastly at an object as if curious to know what it might be. Only such are capable of performing feats of skill.

There is no difference between men and animals in this matter.

The mighty musician is concentrated in his gaze.

The mighty miracle worker is steadfastly attentive to the principles that first attracted him and which make his works successful. The miracles themselves are of little account to the miracle worker. It is the principles which charm him. On the other hand if the miracles themselves charm him and he watches the operation of change from disease to health, from idiocy to intelligence, with concentrated devotion everything will change while he looks at it.

Change from imperfection to perfection is his idea. It penetrates him and is himself. Whatever he looks at must operate to suit him. His idea is alive, strong, workative.

Ideas are now running things in this universe in their own ways.

People who attend them are as much run by them as things are run by them. The question of great importance to answer is: "Is it worth while to be run by an idea?" Since an idea is something that is related in nature, ability, office and result to billions of sisters and brothers, is any idea, however lofty and sublime, worthy to be called God? Should it have the rights of Absolute God?

It is an established fact that an idea will manipulate and manage things its own way if well attended to.

All people are more or less governed by ideas, first one and then another taking possession of them. Are they themselves while being run and manipulated by ideas? Is there something that is not an idea which it is better to be? Are we something when not managed by the best idea ever instituted but nothing when run and manipulated by one?

Is God obliged to select an idea to focus His attention to?

Is God something beyond and independent of ideas? If I am God, into whose hands have I given my throne if I let an idea run me?

It is the old fable of the king who set a fool upon his throne and could not get him off, if I find that I the king have let an idea manage my kingdom. I will do so no longer. I am MYSELF.

I am not controlled by an idea either good or bad, lofty or ignoble.

I am Myself.
I am God.
I am King.
I am what I Am.
I will not be what I am not.
In My presence ideas dissolve.
Now I know.

VI

It is written that when the Lord God takes His seat in the throne all the twenty-four elders shall fall down on their faces, crying "Holy, Holy!" The twenty-four elders are so far as we are concerned the twenty-four lessons concerning God. The Lord God is the Self understanding the self. We are dealing with externals while we are dealing with lessons. When we understand we lay down our lessons.

God hath His seat at the center of our being. When all our nature turns to look upon our God that nature is gone and God is left.

The Eternal One is God. The nature that eats and drinks, that loves and hates, is the temporal one. The temporal has no life of its own, no intelligence of its own, therefore it is called the unreal nature.

Only the eternal Substance is the real Substance. Therefore in all metaphysics we read, "God is the only Substance. God is the only Intelligence."

Self-treatment *Self Treatments*

There is all understanding in God. Every flash of understanding we are conscious of is a reminder that God is nigh us even in our heart and in our mouth.

As the rose gathers all the red of the universe and is red itself so we may be all the understanding of the universe flash by flash. Every religion has for its purpose, expressed or unexpressed, the union of God at our center with the universal God free from delusions, free from temporals[3] as the gardener's purpose is to unite the red focus at the heart of the rose with the red of the empyrean, without mixtures.

Religion acts as a gardener to our red heart love by drawing all the love

---

[3] She uses the term "temporals" to refer to the temporary manifestations that make up most of our experience.

Emma Curtis Hopkins

of God to unite with our love. The temporals of human life are excluded by the pure and undefiled religion.

Love that is pure from the temporals is eternal, absolute God.

Mind pure of temporals is mighty understanding.

Truth that mentions temporals as not real and not operating is the shining power, the irresistible, impregnable God.

Truth that shows its power at once is truth. It waits not an instant. The rose shows its red the instant it is red. The rose lay in the air behind it before it turned its form downward and sprang back again. Is it not written that every plant was created before it appeared?

So thy shining understanding which is thy God heart was all glorious before it turned itself downward into human temporals and slowly regathered itself to its former splendor.

Stand thou upright, O Soul! Hast thy turning into the human ground and flowering altered the red at thy heart?

Hast thou not learned much of the not God by thy human sojourn?

Love is God. Understanding is God. Thy red heart is Love. Thy red heart is God. Thy red heart is understanding. Thy red heart is God. Its name is the Name in the name Jesus Christ. The airs hide the splendors of the living God from thee, but when thou openest thy heart at the teaching of thy Gardener, the religion of union, unity, One, and His name One, the airs will stand aside, they will turn into the fine lights of their original estate like thyself. All nature will break forth at thy understanding of thyself. Thou art that

One that should first discover thyself and in discovering thyself all things discover themselves.

Thou art alone in the universe.
Thou art the Shining One.
Take now thy seat in thy throne.

VII

We are told that there are vibrations streaming through the universe. If we chord with them we are in harmony with our life. All our actions charm our world. All our world's actions charm us. The mind has its fingers with which to touch the fine threads of music that string themselves to and fro. It has eyes to see their twining enchantments.

If we use the mind's fingers first, the external fingers will do all things swiftly and skillfully.

If we use the mind's eyes first, the outer eyes will see all things quickly and truly. The love threads string straight past our doors. The wisdom threads stream close to our sight.

The life threads are strung under our fingers. Truth, power, fearlessness, beauty, prosperity go through our bodies in shining beams and all cross at our heart's center to call our attention.

The Master and King in the Absolute Mind's heart realm having His seat at our heart knows all these lines, and lives in everlasting concord with them. The flesh mind is invited to join in the song, in the strain, in the works of the Spirit. The invitation chants and rechants,

"Come unto me,"
"Sing the new song,"
"O turn ye."

There is no end to its song. We may keep eyes on the flesh, keep fingers on matter through this world, through the next world, through the world beyond that, on into the three heavens of our Bible, the twin heavens of Mohammed, the ten heavens of Dante, we may return again to this planet, or fly to Saturn, Jupiter, Mars, Venus—but the call of the Master and King, the inconceivably small One, the everywhere present One, is still the same! "Come!"

Listen, O ye people!

Listen, O my being! I hear the voice of the King in the garden center, my heart; I will attend to the Spirit from henceforth and forever. I will not know more of the worlds of matter that chime not with the song. Why should I not be what I may be? Why should I not be the song at my heart?

Why should the harmony of the everlasting chords not touch my voice with music so that when I speak my words heal the wounds of creation?

May I not speak from the Spirit within? Is it not written that the words I speak may be the words of the Father that dwelleth within me? What is the difference between Jesus Christ and the man of flesh handling matter with weariness and pain forever?

It is only that He hearkens and does, and thus is alive forevermore with the word of the Master and King, the Father. I am privileged to hearken and do.

I turn my mind's eyes toward Thee, O King, whose everlasting place is within me. Thou callest my Name. Thou callest it again. I am not mistaken. The sound of my own Name opens my ears, my eyes, all my senses. I see

Thee face to face. I can speak Thy language.

VIII

The photographer covers his plates with collodion which makes them negative. They cannot then help receiving the stamp of that which is looking at them.

The whole universe is in the state of that negativized plate. It waits through aeons, changeless negative, for me to stamp my "I Am what I Am" upon it.

One moment's uneasy silence and the "I am that I think I am" is impinged on the negative universe. I do not like it. The experiences are distasteful, unrelishable.

For what I think I am, I am not, by any manner of means. But if I impress upon this universe that which I AM, I then am utterly and absolutely satisfied with what transpires.

Be still, myself—be still. Be still with the calm of the one that I AM. For I would write on the plastic walls of an eternal blank that which I AM that is true; and I have not thought it out, but it was and is and always will be my own glorious being.

I would write on the plastic walls my being's original beauty, my being's pristine goodness, my being's wondrous kindness. Then all the world would be my perfect image.

The subject sits softly still while he prints his image on the collodionized plate. So I will sit still while I imprint the splendor of my God-knowledge, God-beauty, God-power, upon the waiting universe. To myself I will say, "Be still and know that I am God." There is no restlessness in me. I am at peace. I am still. My strength is to sit still. I fill myself with thoughts and then for one moment I preserve a seeming stillness. The reprint of my thoughts and words with which I have covered myself will appear soon in my world. But what I AM, indeed that is not thinkable; that is it which I have a baptism to be baptized with—that is my only call.

I write the splendor of my native genius on the walls of eternity. Then all the mirrored surface shows me splendid genius. Great men, wonderful women, light and peace and beauty, music, song, knowledge, all that Jesus Christ knows, now this day are shown me face to face.

The I Am that has imprinted its thoughts on the walls of eternity is not I. Thoughts are set aside while I am still. The I AM whose words are showing me my past and present and future in the people and the things I meet is not I.

Oh! I AM the wonderful Being before whom cherubim and seraphim fall down forgotten. I must be still and think nothing. I must be still and print the image of myself on the plastic walls that close around me.

At my stillest center I am the undefeatable, unspeakable One. Jesus Christ wrote on the plastic airs his character and none question the stainless splendor of that figure wherever man returns an image thereof.

That Name silences my restless mind. It stills my angry pulse. It puts my energy to sleep. Thus I step one step nearer the silence which can print a universe with goodness, beauty, majesty, power, wisdom. I am the writer of God. What I have written that was not God has fallen into that negative quality into which the air walls are forever resolving themselves. They are fresh each moment for a new image. I am still. I am still. Upon the soft ethers of eternity I hereby print my character, my name, my Self as I AM.

IX

"Thy word was unto me the joy and rejoicing of my heart."

The word of the Lord concerning joy is to be given forth into the world either by pen or thought or speech.

Where is the rejoicing heart? Where is the good news that would make my mouth pleasant with speech and my pen enchanting?

There is good news from somewhere for me to hear.

Who hears the news in his secret mind and will not tell it unto me, which if I heard it would make my heart leap with joy, and brighten my eyes with beautiful smiles? Where is the messenger from the far country whose face bears the news my soul waiteth like a thirsty hart in the desert for, as it longeth for the waters?

Is the news close at my hand?

Is the good nigh me or far off that I am waiting to realize?

Good news from a far country!

Mail from the glad lands!

Messengers from home!

These are my right. God hath all this in His keeping. God hath me in His heart. God hath a way for me as mathematics has a way for its worker to solve his hard problems.

Jeremiah, the sad, sang that the word of the Lord was the joy and rejoicing of his heart. The word of the Lord— the word of the Lord—the word of the Lord. Where is the word of the Lord?

Moses tells me it is nigh me, even in my heart and in my mouth. The word that would make me like a tree of delight by the running rivers is in my mouth.

What matter if I never speak it?

Am I not glad that it is in my heart and in my mouth?

That a priceless treasure I possess— namely, a word which if I spoke, the heaven of heavens could not contain Me.

The whole creation hath in its heart, but giveth not forth, that wondrous treasure.

The whole creation hath a mouth and speaketh not the wondrous message. Speak—speak—speak—mouth!

Strike out thy word from the heart point where the word liveth. Has the word of the mouth of man been divorced from the heart of man?

Speaketh no man from his heart?

This explains why I have not heard you speak the good news I am fainting to hear.

This explains why you have not heard me speak the good news you have languished for while I would not speak it. I will make haste to speak and think and set my seal and sign manual unto, the words that are in my heart and mouth.

I see now the ministry of Truth. I see now the ministry of all religions. It is to unite the tongue and heart. Will not the fingers write what the heart feeleth and the mouth speaketh?

Will not the feet run where the heart and tongue tell?

Is ever the heart satisfied with temporal things?

Wherefore is Martha who has strung her tongue to speak of material ways and her heart to an artificial imagination that changeable structures are its delight, the governor of the homes of the planet? Is she satisfied to be restless alone? Does she not urge that men work and hurry to build and study and beautify what is?

Does the Martha heart, strung out of its central poise, not drive the tongue, the pen, the feet, to save and hoard and arrange knowledge and friends and gold that wealth may be our portion?

Why should Martha rule the world?

Is she not artificial heart and tongue?

How can I stop my agreement with the unpoised heart and tongue? Have I not also been thinking that I ought to do something different from what I am doing or redouble my exertions on the same line in order to accomplish more? Do I not agree in love of things which is no love at all? I will now retire from the strife. I will be my heart as it is strung by itself, swinging its everlasting life in lone beauty and moving my tongue with kindness and rejoicing.

I will not speak and speak and speak of things which are not my heart's joy till I swing a false heart into my days.

I will not draw nigh the Spirit with my lips while that trained heart is far from the Spirit.

The heart and mouth that are at variance I will not use. I will let the true heart and its mouth do all the speaking and thinking.

The heart and tongue that are strung to performing with matter are but shadows. Whoever dwelleth much with them describeth his troubles continually. He is all trouble, all pain, all anxiety. One little taste now and then he getteth of pleasure, but its brief moment hasteth by and he giveth days and nights and days and nights to further vanities of effort for one other taste of pleasure.

But always there back of the shadow swingeth a heart and mouth and tongue with everlasting rejoicing. Singing, singing, as the morning stars, as the bride and bridegroom, as the king and queen in majesty and beauty. These are nigh me even in my heart and mouth. Let them be me. I interfere not.

X

An unreliable presence is the mind that is swayed by alternating feelings of good and evil. While the good feeling inspires a mind it is radiant, buoyant, healthy. While the ill feeling stirs the mind it is gloomy, depressing, disease-breeding.

The external world is made up of the alternating moods of mind.

When a Mohammed puffs and inflates his mind with professions that it with its body is the greatest, the brightest, the ablest that the Lord ever created, the wind that blows from that good feeling is very convincing to the wavering and uncertain other minds around. Other winds have blown feebly one day and strongly the next day which other men's minds have infused them with, be-cause other men were not so well inflated.

They had not stretched the capacity of their *w*indbags to equal extent with the Mohammed type. The Lord that filleth Mohammed with steady conceit and filleth Theudas with wavering conceit is not the Absolute and Impartial Lord Eternal, but the shadow Lord. The shadow Lord is one *Adonai* as the Impartial Lord is One God.

The multitudes of visible men and women are the different creations of the *Adonai*, or Lord of the whole earth. He puffeth Mohammed with conceit and Theudas with conceit and you with conceit and me with conceit in less or greater quantum.

When I hear that I am as great and wonderful of mind as I have courage to affirm I am then being alone with my Lord of the earth, *Adonai*. I then begin at my Lord's orders to say, "I am omnipresent, omnipotent, omniscient."

I repeat many other affirmations, as, "I am free, wise, immortal." Whatever I then say comes into my mind as a potency. I show forth somewhat in my bodily condition like these affirmations. The *Adonai* or my Lord of my earth may confer with himself to make me a Jesus or a Pilate. But this Lord of my life tells me that the highest he knows is that a man's word is his burden or his freedom. The highest he knows is, "Be ye steadfast to goodness." "Be ye speakers of right words." "Be ye aware that the Lord that dealeth with matter and saith unto the flesh, 'To one I give great power and to another small power,' that Lord is nobody and nothing but the human ego."

So the Lord of the whole earth that teacheth men the difference between good and evil is Adonai—the human ego, who is everywhere ruling matter and mind, showing mercy to one man, hardening another man; ennobling one man, belittling another man, at his will. The Bibles of the world are mostly telling of the human ego and calling him Lord, God, Jehovah.

Wherever man or woman or child sees that the human ego or Lord of the earth is the claim of intelligence without being really Intelligence, there is a fine rift made in the shadow and the true Lord is somewhat understood. When the inflated mind is happy and joyous it inflateth and happyfieth other minds. But it is unreliable happiness. So of its gloom.

The shine of the changeless and reliable One, whose name has not been spoken through all teachings, through all feelings is the shine of Changeless Paradise.

XI

One bright glance of understanding through the mind that dealeth with earth, putteth the mind that lordeth it over all the earth quite away.

By one bright glance of the changeless and reliable One through the cloudy mind of human ego the day dawns of which the prophets have prophesied when there should be everlasting joy and beauty in the earth as in heaven.

There is a spot of mind in the midst of mind that knoweth there is something different, different, different, from what human mind telleth, though human mind may be telling angels and archangels in fadeless Paradise. There in that spot is everlasting denial of what is called bliss.

Take notice while the eloquent psalmist repeats lines describing heavenly joys, how, at that spot within thee, there resideth the denier of it all.

The best songs are only echoes though they rouse the heart to loftiest exaltations. Some chord is yet untouched while cherubim and seraphim are pictured as calling thee home, home, home. That untouched chord, that unresponding spot is the God point in thy being.

Let descriptions of Paradise stand aside. What can the cloud know of the sunshine? What can shut eyes know of what is going on around them? What can the Lord of all the dark and changing earth know of Him that dwelleth in bright heaven? The only truth the Lord that maketh thy mind strong or maketh thy body beautiful, can tell thee, that will call thy God point to respond, is "I am nothing!" "Something within thee rouseth as it were to shine when the Lord that created the heavens and the earth telleth the opening truth, "I am nothing! nothing!"

Let the ego repeat this self-dissolving truth till the unresponding spot within thee riseth in its shining gladness and the heavens and the earth hide it no longer from that which it knoweth is true. The Lord that made the heavens and the earth is nothing and less than nothing and all that he hath made is naught. The everlasting denier within thee is not error but truth, is not the devil, but God.

The everlasting denier of all the talk of the beauty and goodness of the saints is the unresponding God point at thy center. It knows that no saint was ever described aright. No heaven with angels and happiness was ever told of, that was rightly told of.

Nothing—nothing—nothing ever pleases that denier, that unconvinced and inconvincible God within thee.

It is against all forms, all ceremonies, all bliss of mind, all gloom, all man, all Bible, all science, everything! It is the worm that dieth not even while Jesus Christ is being taught of. It is the fire that is not quenched while Science telleth of a pathway to God by the living word.

Have thy way, O unresponding, unsatisfied One at my center! Spring forth through my being, through my will, through my mind, through all that I think that pleaseth thee not! Thou shalt shine, thy bright glancing undarkened by my counsel. Thy will be done with me. Thy judgment in its beauty reigneth.

XII

"The words that I speak unto you it is not I that speak, but the Father that dwelleth in me, He doeth the works."

"Believe me for the very works sake."

"If I do not the works of the Father, believe me not."

"An evil and adulterous generation seeketh after a sign, and there shall no sign be given it."

A work is a sign of what has been going on. I look at my photograph and do not like it. But that photograph pictures exactly what was going on when I looked into the camera all collodion. I see a picture of what I did. I am not pleased with my world, but it is all the work of my hands. I looked toward the willing banks of morning ether and they registered me.

Here comes a cripple. He had only ether soft and yielding the instant before I looked at him. I threw that moment an ill projection from my stock of spears.

Creation is new every moment. I will have no words but the words of the Father that dwelleth in me. The Father is the everlasting protestant within me that would imprint Himself in unspeakable splendor on the ethers that fold me.

I will see that the new creation showeth the Father.

Then as thou beholdest the lame walk, the blind see, the ignorant awaken, thou shalt believe me, for the works will testify whose words are going forth. And if I do not cast on the yielding walls around me these signals, thou canst not believe that I am the words of God altogether, for these signs follow them that speak the speech of God.

If I am mournful at sight of evil I am mourning because I have two sides to my thoughts. One side is the everlasting denier of the way I do things, and the other is speaking what I remember of my last creations, and fearing my new creations. To be divided in house is the fall of the house. Division is adultery. How can the photograph picture God if I hide God by a veil of mournful thoughts?

If God is my native glory within me, when I pray, "Thy will be done," is it not the native energy of my own being unto whom I pray? Whose will but my own can be done?

Have I two wills, two natures, two powers, at variance—one ignorant, mournful, incompetent; the other wise, joyful, competent? I see how it is. The ignorant, sad, incompetent, nature is shadow, sham, unreality. Now that I know its character it vanishes.

Knowledge dispels ignorance. Knowledge of joy dispels sadness. Knowledge of ability dispels inefficiency.

The God that is my native glory within me is my God. This God doth not need time to work miracles. If I give Him myself, give myself to my native glory within me, then He hath His own way. My Self hath His way. "My ways are not your ways, saith the Lord."

"Behold I am against thee." And as formerly I thought it took time to break the loaves of bread from one loaf into an hundred through new kneading and more flour, I see that my native glory taketh no time, but saith only, "It is done," and it is done. My God taketh no time to perform wonderful, wonderful things. How glorious art Thou, how mighty, how astonishing to the former ways! I praise and extol Thee, and praising and extolling Thee, all that is unlike Thee, all that is against Thee, disappeareth! I as mortal, incompetent, ignorant, am swallowed up of Immortality, Wisdom, God! I am swallowed up of my Self! Every fiber of me shineth! Every movement of me glorifieth. My raiment is all white and glistening. Every word of me delighteth.

Yet not I, but the Father that dwelleth in me!

Not unto me but unto Thee the glory!

My name shall no more be earth—but Thy name is my name. The earth me hath perished at sight of Thee. I remember not the former me. As a dream when one awaketh so at sight of Thee I forget all but Thee. There are not two of me. There is only One. That one is radiant God.

The New Gospel[4]

---
[4] From *The Gospel Series,* WiseWoman Press, 2006.

I take by choice the thoughts which all the world call the mountain peaks of thought. These are of God, who is finer than understanding of God. I keep them going in the wheeling batteries of my mind. They generate a substance upon which my understanding feeds.

This understanding is hot. It melts my old thoughts and dissolves my old body. It then takes new thoughts of God. And beyond itself generates a newer substance so white—fuller and whiter than anything on earth. A finer and clearer understanding breaks forth. It speaks and I see what body God created. I am in the understanding of God.

This is rest. This is the rest of God. It is action so swift that it is no action at all. I seem to be doing nothing. I seem to be thinking nothing. But my fine true thoughts heating my understanding till it dissolves thoughts is swiftly putting me into my transfigured body of God. It is by Spiritual Science reasonings that I generate that substance which feeds understanding.

...

My God is Omnipresent, Omnipotent, Omniscient Good. My God is Life filling earth and sky and stars beyond stars. There is no point of space or place that My God with His Life unchecked, unhindered, is not eternally present. My life is God, filling all the pathways of the universe. Nothing can take away Life as nothing can take away God. Let Life now be manifest everywhere and in everything, according to this Truth. All is Life Omnipresent, Omnipotent, Omniscient.

Emma Curtis Hopkins

My God is Truth. Truth fills all places and spaces and atoms and objects and thoughts of Omnipresence. All things are filled with Truth and tell Truth only.

...

Affirmations[5]

---

[5] From *The Gospel Series,* WiseWoman Press, 2006.

First:

My Good is my God, Omnipresent, Omnipotent, Omniscient. My Good is my Life. My Good is my Truth. My Good is my Love. My Good is my substance.

Second:

I am my own idea of God and according to my idea of God, I live, move and have my being.

Third:

I am Spirit-Mind, like my God, and I reflect Wisdom, Strength, Holiness.

Affirmations   *Self Treatments*

Fourth:

My God works through me to will and to do whatever ought to be done by[6] me.

Fifth:

I am governed by my God and cannot sin, cannot suffer for sin, nor fear sin, sickness or death.

Sixth:

I am beloved.

Seventh:

I am at peace with all the world.

---

[6] In today's language, this would be "whatever is my fulfillment to do."

Forgiveness[7]

---
[7] From *Resume,* WiseWoman Press, 2007.

Here is my mind. I spread it out before Thee. Forgive Thou its foolishness and ignorance with Thy bright wisdom. Here is my life. I offer it to Thee. Forgive Thou its contrariness to Thee. Here is my heart. It is Thine only. Forgive Thou its restlessness and dissatisfaction. Forgive its discouragements. Forgive its resentments. Forgive its loves and its hates, its hopes and its fears. Here is my body. I cast it down before Thee. Forgive Thou its imperfection with Thy perfection. Forgive me altogether with Thyself. Give for myself Thyself. So only can I know that:

Thou art, and there is none beside Thee, in Thine own Omnipresence, Omnipotence, Omniscience—

I am Thine only and in Thee I live, move, and have being—

I am Thine own substance, power, and light, and I shed abroad wisdom, strength, holiness, from Thee—

Thou art now working through me to will and to do that which ought to be done by me—

I am forgiven and governed by Thee alone, and I cannot sin, I cannot suffer for sin, nor fear sin, sickness or death.

A New Covenant[8]

---

[8] From *Scientific Christian Mental Practice*, DeVorss, 2006. This is from Lesson Four, on Faith, and would normally be repeated on Thursday morning.

I hereby covenant with the Holy Spirit for my life, and I will do nothing to preserve my life; my life is the Life of Spirit.

I covenant with the Holy Spirit for my health, and I will do nothing to preserve my health; my health is the Health of the Spirit.

I covenant with the Holy Spirit for my strength, and I will do nothing to preserve my strength; my strength is the Strength of the Spirit.

I covenant with the Holy Spirit for my support, and I will do nothing to preserve my support; my support is the Support of the Spirit.

I covenant with the Holy Spirit for my defense, and I will do nothing to preserve my defense; my defense is the protection of Holy Spirit.

I covenant with the Spirit for my mind in its perfect thinking, and I will do nothing for my thoughts; my mind is the Mind of Spirit.

I covenant with the Spirit for my right speech, and I will do nothing for my words; my speech is the Voice of Spirit.

I will do nothing to fix or record or write my Truth unto the earth, for my record is the record of the Holy Spirit. I say, as Job said, "My witness is in the heavens and my record is on high."

I covenant for my joyous song of life, and I will do nothing to be joyful; my joy is the Joy of Spirit.

I covenant with the Spirit for my demonstrations of efficiency and skill in rightly doing all things; my efficiency is the working Skill of Spirit; according to the words of Jesus Christ, who said, "The words that I speak unto you I speak not of myself, but the

Father that dwelleth in me, he doeth the works."

I covenant for my judgment in beauty, and I will do nothing to be greatly good in judgment; for the Spirit is my judgment.

I covenant with the Holy Spirit for my love, and I will do nothing to make myself loving or beloved, for all is the Holy Spirit now acting with irresistible goodness through me.

I do believe that my God is now working in me and through me and by me, to make me omnipotent, omnipresent, and omniscient. I have faith in God. I have the faith of God.

The Radiant I AM[9]

---
[9] Reproduced from the journals of Emma Curtis Hopkin

The listening disciple becomes a preaching apostle. Standing at the Center of Being and looking outward over the world, instruction is received from every quarter. But who hath told himself that all the objects he beholds and all their movements also are but projections of his own judgment? He seems always to be a learner and a seeker till at the center of his consciousness the fact is suddenly proclaimed that he himself produced the world as it appears.

Then he no longer listens to informations from without; he authorizes from himself what he would see and hear and touch; even what he would know.

I have been a listening disciple. I have let people and objects and activities come toward me and impinge upon me till I have been over-piled and mountain-covered with thoughts. But now I know that I AM, at my own Center, authority over and through my universe, and I shall ordain my twelve disciples, or my twelve powers, to spread my Original Nature abroad till from me to the utmost stretches all is my Divine *Ego*.

It is the teaching that all is Spirit, and matter is but obedient shadow-picturing thereof, which is the final subtle message toward me that makes me see that I AM what I AM and alter not. Spirit is the gentle Mother doctrine among the doctrines of the world—gentle but inexorable. She brings to exposure the Man Child, my I AM—who shall rule all nations with a rod of iron. The iron that is strongest is magnetic. It rules in the earth by holding all the particles together. It rules in the sun. It rules in all the spheres. They roll because of the magnet. So all my being has moved because of my I AM. So all my universe shall wheel to my ordination.

This is my ministry. I am glad to give myself to my Self and to give all my world to my Self and let my Self do in judgment twelve works upon the earth.

This is my ministry. I have heard all I shall ever hear. I know all I shall ever know. I now make my Self known.

I make my Self known by speaking, thinking, writing and living the word of my Self—my I AM. I reign from sea to sea and from the river to the uttermost parts of the earth. I reign by my knowledge of my own I AM and its last name. The name of my I AM in the last days of the manifestation of a universe, which I made by not speaking from my Central Point, is Jesus Christ. The I AM in me is Jesus Christ. I speak boldly of my Self to the world in which I walk. I think from my Self forward over its surface through all its substance. I write what I know and I write what I AM, and what I write is the fiber of all things. They shall feel themselves knitting into transfigured embodiments by my written words. "Write what thou hearest and give it unto the churches."

I live as a breath of life forward and back through the universe. I AM the conduct of my world. What I do it does. Conducting from my Center, I satisfy my world with what I AM. My world can find no flaw in Me. I can find no flaw in my Self. Because I live at my Center, ye live also. My rod of iron is my being what I AM and knowing it.

"We give Thee thanks, O Lord God Almighty, because Thou has taken to Thyself Thy great power and hast reigned!" These that are thankful are my powers. I AM Lord God Almighty to my own powers.

I AM the power of Life to the universe. Because I live, all that hath form or name shall live. There shall be no death nor fear of death throughout the boundaries of eternal spaces from this day forth forever. That which proceedeth forth from Me is Life and the power of Life forever. As I breathe, the creatures of the sea and air and sands rise up refreshed and there is no power against their life and no ending of their life forever from this day forth.

I AM the unending, irresistible Life of the world. I think this—I speak this—I write this—I live this. This is my ministry which I AM. "Let us give ourselves to the ministry of the Word."

I AM the power of Health to the universe. Because I AM holy at my Center, I make whole wherever I decree. I AM authority. There shall be happy, joyous, free, fearless Health through this universe from this day. All that have name and shape shall this day lift up their heads with new refreshment. The elixirs of a fadeless healing shall steal through them. There shall be no disease or sickness from this day of the Lord onward. "The inhabitants shall not say, 'I am sick,' any more."

I AM the unending, irresistible, beautiful Health of the whole universe, I, its Center, shed my Health abroad. This is my stopless ministry. I think this—I speak this—I write this—I live this.

Emma Curtis Hopkins

I AM the power of Strength to the universe. Because I AM unalterable, I AM Omnipotence. I minister to myself abroad. All that have shape or name feel stealing through them a reviving Strength from this day which nothing shall ever interfere with. I strengthen wherever I decree. I AM Authority. There shall be lifting up and strong godliness throughout all mysteries of height and depth and plain and valley from this day onward. There shall no faintness seize upon anything. There shall no weakness touch anything. There shall no feebleness be heard of forever and forever. The prophecy is fulfilled in me which reads: "When men are cast down, thou shalt say, there is lifting up."

I Am the Strength of the universe. This is my ministry. Strength that proceedeth from me is irresistible, unending. I think this—I speak this—I write this—I live this. I AM a tower whose radiance is elixir for infinity.

I AM the power of Support to the universe. Everything that hath shape or name is upborne and prospered in all its ways from this day on. There shall be no lack or disappointed effort. All shall rise and have self-respect from this day on. I, from my Center, AM a radiance of unbearing sustainment through all this universe. There shall be no poverty, no lack, no want from this day forth.

I AM the sufficiency of my universe. It is my decree. The elixir of bounty, of prospering effort, spreads forth from me. This is my irresistible unending ministry. I think this—I speak this—I write this—I live this.

I AM a tower whose radiance sheds abroad Protection for infinite kingdoms. That which speeds forth as my radiance is the Holy Spirit of Revelation. I AM the unending peaceable defense of the whole universe. By Me all that have name or shape are safe and secure running, or walking, or flying forever. They shall not fear. They shall not be attacked. They shall not be hurt. The days of hurting have flown away. The dreams of danger are past. Things wake as my mighty elixirs spread through them borne on the streams of my word, my thought, my writings, my life breaths, They rouse themselves. They are safe forevermore. "They shall not hurt or kill in all my holy mountain."

I AM the Security of the infinite stretches and of the near creations. "Peace, peace to them that are afar off and to them that are near." This is my ministry. I think this—I speak this—I write this—I live this.

I AM the power of Mind to my universe. Even the stones shed a message intelligible to all other shapes and names because of my being the Intelligence of all things, shedding my nature forth without stopping. No foolishness or ignorance shall ever shame anything visible or invisible from this day on forever. Its Presence is its wisdom. Its Presence is its information. An elixir of intelligence is on its stopless march from me at my Center forever through all the reaches of space and formulation. I decree Intelligence. I decree Mind. I think and all the universe thinks divinely like Me. My Mind is not as the former mind, which could change or stop. It is the Jesus Christ Mind whose word shall not pass away.

Emma Curtis Hopkins

I AM a tower whose radiance is unending Wisdom through all things. This is my ministry. My logos. I think this—I speak this—I write this—I live this. I AM the radiant Logos in Mind.

I AM the power of Speech to my universe. My tongue is its tongue. What I say, it says from its smallest atom to its gigantic formulation. My Central Name is my tongue of radiance. All that speak, speak of the I AM. One tongue only shall speak. Its language no man or stone did hear nor could ever hear till I should speak from my Center. I now speak what I speak from my Jesus Christ Name. So atoms and angels speak a new heaven and a new earth into their own view, empowered by my tongue with its elixirs of fire. I speak and the universe uttereth itself.

I AM a tower whose radiance sheds eloquent Speech through atoms and men. This is my ministry. I think this—I speak this—I write this—I live this.

I AM the power of Writing—Recording—Witnessing of Jesus Christ and the Name folded within the gates of that Name. What I write the world writes. I fix my hallowed glory with my fingers and all things fix themselves to go no more away from their home forever. The Written Word is the haven of man and of beast. I AM the inspiring pen of the world. I shall find my inspiration everywhere. Nothing unlike my writing lives. I AM from my Center the fixing and transfixing pen. I shall not faint or fail to fix my glory everywhere. I AM man's inspiration with his pen and I inspire all things to record me as I AM.

I AM a tower whose radiance is the inspiration to pen itself in its divinity in every shape and name through infinity. I think this—I speak this—I write this—I live this.

I AM the power of Song—joyous Song that steals in unquenchable smiling through the universe. I AM the Eternal Smile. As I shed my Self through the atoms and through the globes, they sing. I AM the joyous song, unquenchable, unhinderable forever. No other sound but singing, no other voice but joy is heard from this day forth.

I AM the inspiring Joy of my world forever. This is my ministry. I think this—I speak this—I write this—I live this. There is joy beyond ecstasy. I AM that Joy.

I AM the power of Skill for all things. From me there steals forever a quick touch of skillfulness through all fingers. No child needs to be schooled, no bird needs a teacher, no angel needs a helper. All can do their part and they can do what they will to do. There is no incompetency or need of learning from this day on forever, anywhere.

I AM a tower whose radiance is a skill-inspiring elixir, stopless—eternal. This is my ministry. I think this—I speak this—I write this—I live this.

I AM the power of Beauty and Judgment. From my poised place I AM the poise of the ages of men. I judge, and my judgment is what all things go by. They judge like me. I set the features of things into balance and this is their beauty. I balance the atoms that flow in the skin and its balance is its beauty. I set the inner parts into harmony by being the central judgment of eternal facts. I decree and there is no injustice. Nothing falls into mistake. Nothing is unjust. The scales of my judgment are the scales in the hearts of all men. They will not fail to use these scales. And thus order and beauty reign from Pole Star to Southern Cross and from right-hand to left of the worlds beyond worlds. "He shall not faint or fail till He hath established judgment in the earth!" I AM a scale whose rods are the beams of unbreakable right. My judgment is right judgment. As I judge, so it is.

All the poise that I AM I radiate through all the universe and all things feel the joy of adjustment. This is my ministry. This is my nature. I think this—I speak this—I write this—I live this.

I AM the power of Heaven to every atom and to every archangel. From my Jesus Christ center of Being I shed Heaven through the spaces. All things breathe of my radiance. I shed my Self abroad in unending beauty; Heaven breaks in the heart and on the vision from me to all things, through all things. The old heaven and earth sink away into forgotten dreams because I have found my Self, because I know my Self, because I AM my Self. I have taken up the authority I had from before the worlds were spun on the ethers of time.

I decree Heaven and Heaven it is. My Kingdom is come and it is the new land of delight that steals on the vision and reaches the senses of all things. Nothing like the dreams of earth, nothing like the motions of matter ever reaches my universe. As silently as a moonbeam lights on a mountain, so silently has Heaven stolen on the gazes of all the creations of infinity.

I AM a tower whose elixirs of radiance reveal the visions of Heaven to the senses of man. From my Jesus Christ center I AM Heaven from this day forth to all the universe. This is my stopless everlasting ministry. I do this. I AM this. My Name is a folding gate that opens and there is no sound. My Name is Jesus Christ, and in that Name I Am the Heaven of all this universe.

Its meaning is its influence. I AM its meaning, its influence, its heavenliness. I think this—I speak this—I write this—I live this. I AM what I AM. I do what I AM by knowing my Self as Jesus Christ the Heaven-sending Center of Being, the Heaven-sending Me.

NOTES:

RELATED TITLES

by Emma Curtis Hopkins

- First Lessons
- Class Lessons of 1888
- Scientific Mental Practice
- Genesis Series
- Gospel Series
- Judgment Series
- Bible Lessons Series
- High Mysticism
- Resumé
- Esoteric Philosophy

Find these and more information about the "teacher of teachers" at

www.emmacurtishopkins.org

From the WiseWoman Press

Vision Statement:

…To develop, publish, and distribute products of the highest quality that facilitate humanity's transformation …

…To empower and inspire readers to embody their full capacities…

…To be divinely guided and inspired in all that we say and do…

WiseWoman Press

Is an imprint of Portal Center Press
www.portalcenterpress.com

www.ingramcontent.com/pod-product-compliance
Lightning Source LLC
Chambersburg PA
CBHW030527080526
44586CB00011B/352